MW01487714

Unplanned:

Finding Hope After Teen Pregnancy

Blanca Garcia

Unplanned:

Finding Hope After Teen Pregnancy

Published by MBG Publishing
© 2018, Blanca Garcia. All Rights Reserved
Photo credits: Ricky Reyna Jr., Marc Garcia
Cover design: MBG Publishing
ISBN: 978-0-9884703-9-2

For young mothers
in difficult places.

ACKNOWLEDGEMENTS

It takes a village to write and publish a book. I am grateful for all the support I received along the way.

Marc you are the best man I know. Thank you for loving me well and bringing me alongside you to experience greatness. Your support means everything.

Ricky you are weaved into the deepest places of my heart. It is my privilege to love you and call you my son. Whatever our family had to go through, you were worth it. Always.

Mami no hay palabras para agradecer tu sacrificio y amor. Me has enseñado que el amor no se rinde.

My closest friends Yadira LaGuerre and Janice Gamble, you didn't just proofread, you discerned my heart. You have been my cheerleaders and doulas. You also get my humor and accept my awkwardness, which is a major plus. Love you much.

Liz Mitchell and Lenna Fox Smith, thank you for investing your time and expertise. You both made me dig deeper. The work each of you do in our community is life-giving and this generation is better because of it.

The Cordero Family, thank you for taking me in and treating me like one of your own. I always carry with me the example you set of love and family.

Last but not least, God. My breath, my rock, my song. I know you are intimately familiar with my voice. You have translated my tears and my laughter over the years when words were not enough. You're the best! Take this book wherever it is needed cause an outbreak of hope. I know you can. I believe you will.

Contents

1

Runaway

High school can be filled with such an ocean of emotions. I remember a time when I was 11 and my mom took me to a beach. I had been to other beaches before, but this was intimidating. Basic swimming was not a problem for me. This required an experience I did not yet have. Slowly, I would ease into the water then freeze when the wave came. I found myself in that awkward spot where it was too late to turn back, and I was too scared to dive in through it. Eventually the wave would crash right over me and fling me around like a piece of laundry in a washing machine. I would eventually return to the surface alive and slightly traumatized. It was a crazy mix of "I survived!" and "Let's do it again!" The teen years can feel like this. We doggie paddle furiously through an ocean of unfamiliar hormones, as we learn about relationships and trust. At times, the waves of emotions roll through steady and safe. Then without notice, our emotions can turn on us. They become like unpredictable waves and we are left tossed and confused. During these years we try not to drown in the opinions of the popular kids. We also live frustrated because our parents just don't get it. What is "it" by the way? Our clothes, our music, our relationships, our need to get noticed?

We have favorite songs that we play like the soundtrack of our lives. They are the anthems that represent the experiences and bonds we have with other people. Personally, my soundtrack was loaded with freestyle, hip-hop and R&B of the 90s. Music influences our moods and ideas of love. Even today, there are lyrics will randomly pop up in my brain. For my generation there will always be a group of people that will wave their hands in the air "...and wave 'em like they just don't care!" Additionally, movies also have a way of shaping our fantasies and thoughts about romance. We set our expectations based on 90 minutes of great scenes, perfect make-up and scripts. Then once it is over, we encounter real life situations and are surprised by real life disappointments. And it sucks.

At 17, I was a high school senior on Long Island, New York. Real life for me meant being the only daughter of a single mom from Mexico that always hustled to make sure we were taken care of. I was a first-generation American, that didn't seem to always fit in on the American side or the Hispanic side. As an average student I confess that I dreaded reading and passed my math classes by the skin of my teeth. As a bilingual child, my mom depended on me to translate at the store, the doctor's office or at school. She trusted me and did not know that I was sneaky enough to translate the messages to suit my needs. The whereabouts of my father were unknown. Except for one picture that existed, I never knew him, and we never talked about him. My reputation may have been one as a "good girl" because I had managed to stay out of the party scene, and sleeping around. At that time, I worked at the local library after school. There was great pride in earning my own money that I could do with it what I wanted. It was my attempt at independence. I enjoyed hanging out with my friends. They were fun to be around, and I knew they had my back. They were mischievous but not dangerous. I carried strong opinions but out of my group, I was mostly known for being a quiet girl. My mom used to say "Calladita te ves mas bonita," (you look prettier when you are quiet.) Being the quiet girl meant I learned how to be a good listener. Occasionally it also meant I felt invisible. I paid attention to how guys and girls spoke about each other. Guys could be straight forward, sometimes raw. It was based on what I heard, that I decided I was not going the be an "easy" girl. If a guy wanted to get with me, I was going to make it difficult.

In high school teen pregnancy was rare, but it did happen. Once, I remember I looked at a pregnant student and thought, "I will never let that happen to me." According to the stats published by the Centers for Disease Control and Prevention, in 1993 teenage pregnancy rates were slowly dropping. The year I had my baby according to their records, I became part of the 505,488 teens between the ages of 15-19 that gave birth in the U.S.

During my senior year I had my first serious relationship. It was that crazy kind of mix between happy and exhausting. It changed everything.

The story really starts in middle school. I had moved from a large Mexican community in a suburb outside of New York City to Long Island. My self-esteem was low because I was new and feeling like an outsider. The Spanish-speaking community in my new town was mostly Puerto Rican and it felt different. Believe it or not, all Spanish-speakers do not share the same culture and traditions. Add to the mix a bad perm and an intense awareness of my hairy arms. Wow. I shaved them once but could not decide which was worse: arms with hair or arms with stubbles. Somehow, I made peace with the arms I was given.

After having survived the 7th grade in a new school, I was finally comfortable in my surroundings and the familiar faces. Seeing any new kid would have caught my attention. When I began the 8th grade I was feeling confident, and that's when one new face caught my eye.

He made me lose interest in all the other boys. I thought someone that fine had to be the whole package, right? After all, that is what the movies told me. He sported homemade tattoos and always acted like he knew what he was talking about. His presence turned heads and he seemed to know it. At first glance, there was no way to know the layers of his story, but I was determined to find out for myself. Quickly, our circle of friends began to overlap and within a month I found myself hanging out at his house with my friends. By now he had a girlfriend, but I did not care. I took any opportunity to be close by. There were moments it felt like he was giving me special attention. It was enough to keep me coming back and hoping for something more.

We kept in touch on and off through the next few years. We even attempted having a relationship but that was short lived. His attention was such a high that I gave him my virginity. I gave him something that no one else would ever have! Even after that, it did not become anything serious like I had expected. I was let down. He was the bad boy that the girls had their eye on and hoped to tame. He made breaking the rules look cool. With him there was access to beer and a car. Having no license did not stop him from driving. He was making his own rules along the way and that was magnetic to the people around him, including me. People would always wonder what he was going to do next.

> "It felt good to have someone this protective over me."

When he started paying attention to me again in my senior year, I could not believe it! Privately, he was different with me than with everyone else. I could see a tender side. It made me feel special, like I had unlocked a hidden part of his heart. That is a powerful feeling, addictive even.

He lived in New Jersey by then with a family he knew since childhood. On the weekends, he would make the drive to see me. This seemed to scream to me "You're important!" He cared about me, where

I went and who I was with. He even discouraged me from having guy friends. It was sweet to think that he was afraid to lose me, and it made me feel even more valuable. It felt good to have someone this protective over me.

This "protectiveness" was really a major red flag called jealousy, I just did not know it then. It started off as sweet. Keep in mind though, jealousy comes from a place of insecurity and is not healthy for either person. Jealousy will destroy a relationship when left unchecked.

Quickly, it was clear that he did not get along with my friends and I felt torn. Emotionally, I was walking on eggshells. Trying to please him and them was wearing me out. This was new territory that I had not expected. One time, we all tried to go out together and had to cut the night short because of the tension between us all. They were lighthearted, and he was intense. It felt awkward. After that, I was either with him or I was with them, but we couldn't all be together. Still, I was finally the one in a serious relationship. In my logic, it was worth the sacrifice.

As a single parent, my mom did her best. One thing she could not be was a man. I had no strong loving male influence in my life and it left me vulnerable. There was no healthy example of how a man should treat a woman and novelas (Spanish soap operas) did not cut it. As a child, I used to get asked by other children how it felt not to know my father. How does one answer that? How can you miss what you never had? It was not until years later that I learned of the effects of growing up fatherless. Without a father figure, I had no healthy model to show me that a man stays, loves and protects.

At home, the boundaries were not clearly set, and my mom was losing control. His visits turned into overnight weekend visits. This was a recipe for disaster and gave way to the sexual part of our relationship. Know this, whether you are married or not, the reality is that sex creates a bond between two people. In a healthy relationship, it can be a beautiful thing. For us, that would not be the case.

One night, my new official boyfriend met me after work to walk me home. Just like in the movies, we talked, laughed and enjoyed the beautiful fall night. On the way, we saw some friends of mine, all guys. I started to feel the tension build up. One of them shared a quick "Hi" as we passed. I thought I could finally breathe. We got a few steps ahead when my boyfriend's jealousy got the best of him. In true roughneck style he decided to go back to confront them. He did not shy away from giving someone a "beat down" even if he was outnumbered. Our romantic walk home turned into chaos and by the end of the confrontation he had assaulted one of them with a boxcutter. Would it surprise you to know my boyfriend was on parole at the time for a prior incident? This was bad. Really bad.

In a moment, my life turned upside down. Later that night, I felt pressured to choose between him and everything else. This kicked off a series of bad decisions like abandoning my job, dropping out of school, running away from home, and being nearly homeless multiple times.

Leaving seemed like a legit option at first. During my high school years my mom would threaten to send me to a girls group home when our fighting became too much for her. There was one down the street from us, so her threat felt real. Her words cut me deeply. It always left me feeling stunned and confused. Who does that! That is why leaving became an option. I moved with him to New Jersey, and even enrolled in school. It was a joke. I kept falling asleep in class and no one at my new school knew what was going on. We tried to make the situation normal, and even invited my mom to a Thanksgiving dinner.

Shortly after, we got word that a NY detective was attempting to contact us. We wondered how they knew where we were. We got scared and ran, again.

We went to New York's Penn Station, so we could leave using the Greyhound bus and rode through the states on the East coast. We made a few temporary stops in North Carolina for a couple of weeks, before ending up in Texas. It was fun at first, because it felt adventurous. We started out with enough money to stay in decent motels that were the least expensive. On a few occasions, large public fountains where people would throw their coins in for good luck provided us with water. Pecan trees close to one of our motel spots gave us free snacks. We had an unsuccessful attempt at getting into a local homeless shelter because I was not old enough. The last thing we wanted was to draw attention from the police. There were times that we did not know what we would eat or where we would lay our head at night. My great adventure had gone terribly wrong and what began as exciting turned sour quickly. He eventually found an old family friend that lived several cities away and we stayed with her for a few weeks. It was safe there.

Our relationship became a continual cycle of drama, violence and being lovey-dovey again. I started to believe the lie, that if I hadn't done this or said that, then he would not have reacted that way. The truth is, every person is in control of themselves. I am responsible for how I think, what I say and how I act. Listen to me, only powerless people are out of control. Only powerless people say, "You made me do it."

When we added alcohol to the mix, a bad situation turned worse. The bruises told a story I was not willing to tell. Our sexual relationship did not help, it only clouded our judgment. In my immaturity, it formed an unhealthy loyalty to him. I was so addicted to the attention he gave me, that I was willing to sacrifice myself for it. I did not realize the price I was paying.

We became beggars. Once, we almost slept under a bridge when the money had run out. We heard the voices of two guys walking close by that freaked us out and we left. Next, we tried knocking on doors from house to house on a cold night, asking if we could find refuge in a garage or shed. Somehow, I was volunteered to be the one to knock and ask. I was so embarrassed. At this one house we stumbled upon, there was a family gathering. Close to the front door, I could see they were happily huddled around the TV, probably for a football game. I still remember the stunned looks on their faces as I stood there with our humble request. Here I was, asking for something I already had at home. I felt so ashamed. They turned us down and we left on to the next house. Minutes later, they came to find us in a car. We did not know what to think. While they could not give us a place to stay, they had all pitched in their money, so we could have a motel for the night. God bless that family, wherever they are today!

Money and resources started to dry out and when we decided to head for Texas. It seemed like the next best idea since my boyfriend had family there. Keep in mind, we were paranoid and still running from the police. At some point, I had managed to convince my mom to join us. I was living a twisted fantasy, thinking my mom would relocate and we could start a new life. Really, what we wanted was for her to fund our foolishness. She agreed to make the trip most likely because she was starving for a relationship with me. I was the only family she had left and was gone from home at this point for over a month. My mom was willing to take this risk to see me. She did not know what she was walking into and her visit proved to be an eye-opening experience. My mom saw her only daughter falling apart in a controlling and abusive relationship. She never saw him hit me. What she had seen were the bruises that I was good at explaining away. Eventually she started to put all the pieces together. No parent wants their child to live this. I was in a relationship that was like a shaky roller coaster, going fast on unstable tracks. Whether I liked it or not, there was a bond and I could not manage to let go.

The day I found out I was pregnant we were temporarily staying in yet another motel. A missed period was overlooked in all our shenanigans and secretly we began to wonder. My boyfriend and

I snuck away to a local pharmacy and built up the nerve to buy a pregnancy test. It was so awkward. Sometimes you just don't believe it until you see it in black and white, or in our case + (positive) or - (negative). I remember coming back to the motel room and heading straight for the bathroom to follow the test kit instructions. Waiting for the results felt like an eternity. I think every woman feels this way, no matter what the circumstances are. I remember seeing the faint pink sign start to form... to positive. I was indeed pregnant. In that moment, it felt like time stood still.

> "It turns out this baby would be my saving grace."

It was like when you hit the pause button on the dramatic part of a movie. Without any outside influence, my first immediate thought was "I am not getting an abortion." Back then, I could not have told you where I drew the strength to decide that all by myself. As bad as things were, I knew this was not an option. My next thought was, if my mom could do it, I could do it. In me, was this idea that babies are meant to be cared for, not abandoned.

It turns out this baby would be my saving grace. Sometimes parents make sacrifices for their children that they would not do for themselves. I did not have the strength to leave the destructive relationship I was in, yet for the sake of my new baby, I started to think about a better life. I vaguely remember my boyfriend being shocked and surprisingly happy. The idea of fatherhood appeared to affirm his manhood. All I could think about next was how I would tell my mom. What would she think? How would she react? How would this change us?

It took my mom a few days to get back to rational thinking before she prepared her return home. She was on a line of passengers waiting to board the Greyhound bus when I decided to tell her. Listen, there was no perfect time. Telling her was going to be difficult no matter what. We were saying goodbye in a crowd of strangers when I whispered the news in her ear. There was no reaction, no words, just a blank stare. My guess is that she was in shock too. She did not even fight for me to come with her. She chose what therapists call "tough love," and she let me be. She understood that no matter how much she would try to hold me back, I would eventually find a way to leave again. My mom knew me, and she was right. After years of life experience and motherhood, I now recognize how hard that was for her. It was true. I was stubborn and had to learn for myself.

There I was, a pregnant high school drop out with no job and no plans. To anyone looking at me and my situation, it must have looked hopeless. Yet, the baby growing inside me was a little seed of hope. Something to look forward to. Someone to live for.

Our money ran out again and it forced us to stay at the home of one of my boyfriend's family members in the area. We were back in a cycle of drama, violence and being lovey-dovey again. I thought I could be enough for him, but alcohol was my rival. I tried to cope the best I could. Life became about two main things: throwing up or sleeping to escape my circumstances. I learned that if I was asleep then he would leave me alone. In moments when there was no threat of violence, I still chose to become violent. His way of life had become my way of life. I have this one vivid memory of a time when I felt threatened and got so bold I threw the first punch. I met him face to face and hit him square in the jaw. He was so stunned it made him laugh. Ironically, my reaction lightened the mood. I was left completely confused. I was like a scared animal that had been cornered one too many times. I only lasted a couple of more weeks there and it became crystal clear. It was time for me to leave.

Deep down inside I came to myself. Like a boxer who had been knocked out, finally "came to," and got up. It was an awakening. I could see I was in a dangerous relationship with an emotionally unstable person. I trusted him to protect me from the rest of the world, and yet he could not protect me from himself. I wanted to feel safe again. I needed to feel safe again.

People say, "It's always the quiet ones." Yes, I was still the quiet girl, but I was in survival mode and my mind was racing on the inside. One decision set my plan in motion. I set him up with a distraction and snuck away from the house. Hoping his family would not notice, I went speed walking down the street as fast as I could. Running would have been too dramatic and besides I needed to save what little energy I had. I left with the clothes on my back, just a little money and no identification. Over 1,600 miles from home, I was scared and played everything by ear.

At a local fast food spot, I managed to get a taxi and laid low in the back seat. A sense of power and safety started to come back to me. It was hard to trust anyone at this point, but the taxi driver was so kind. He was an older gentleman that talked to me about his family. I was shocked to learn that his wife's family was from the same town that I belonged to in New York! It felt like a sign from God and it gave me peace. That was enough to make me feel safe to share with him why I needed to get home.

We made our first stop at the closest police station, and they redirected us to a smaller law enforcement office. While there, I specifically asked the detective for help to call my mom because I wanted her to know my story was for real. Just weeks before, I had lied to get more money only to keep us on the run. This time was different, the runner in me was tired. I felt responsible to assure her that this time she could wait for me to come home and I would be there. She did not hesitate to send me help. The driver dropped me off at the bus station and wished me the best. God bless him, he helped to save a life that night.

Within walking distance, I was able to pick up the money my mom had sent through Western Union. I found a local fast food place to eat and rested. It was already dark, and the area was sketchy, but I didn't care. I was high on power. Once I got back to the bus station, I kept alert and hid in the women's bathroom until it was time to board.

It must have been hell on earth for my mom. For periods of time she did not know where her daughter was or if she would ever see her again. Her trust had been betrayed and her money had been misused.

Only two months earlier, I had left home with great excitement and high hopes. Now, I was coming back with my heart broken, literally sick and tired. I had a bad case of morning sickness and a lack of food had left me weak. Thank God for saltine crackers and Arizona Iced Tea! It was how I survived the first few months of my pregnancy.

Instead of choosing to stay stuck in my mess, I began to look up and envision my future. What made the difference was that little seed of hope growing in me. That became the reason I could see the future. Motherhood was starting to look and feel like the promise of a new life.

Would you come and sit with me for a moment to rest your soul? I created a section like this for you at the end of each chapter because I know there is a lot going on in your life right now.

Let's take it one step at a time. Just breathe.

It may be hard to tell someone else how you feel if you do not yourself. You can take baby steps by taking time to identify how you feel. Self-awareness is a gift you can give yourself today. Would you agree?

Below, circle as many words as you need to,
that identify how you are feeling right now:

Angry	Determined	Lost	Safe
Anxious	Disappointed	Loved	Scared
Ashamed	Embarrassed	Nervous	Stupid
Brave	Excited	Peaceful	Surprised
Calm	Happy	Proud	Thankful
Confident	Hopeful	Regretful	Trapped
Confused	Insecure	Sad	Worried

2

Determined

The trip back home felt so long. After not being sure of what to expect, my mom welcomed me with open arms and put to rest my anxieties. After such stressful traveling, it was like breathing life into me. I laid down my pride and received the love that I had known since birth. My mom did not shame me. Even with all her flaws and dysfunctions, I do not ever remember feeling judged by her. I was so grateful I could come back home.

Correct me if I am wrong. Leaving Texas so suddenly seemed like a pretty clear break-up message to me. Was it not? A few days after coming home, my now ex-boyfriend came looking for me. His return was scary for two reasons: First, I did not know what he would do. Secondly, I did not know if I would be strong enough not to take him back again. He called my name through the window and I could hear the pain in his voice. He was sorry. I wish I could tell you it didn't matter and that I didn't care. Even though he had hurt me, I also knew he was capable of being kind and funny. It was so hard to stick to my decision.

I knew he was taking a risk of being arrested again just by being back in New York. Remember, he had violated his parole there by assaulting my friend.

Not sure of what to do, I called one of my best friends for help. She and her dad came to pick me up in the middle of the night. They took me back to their house where I hid out for several days. Their home became a safe space for me, and their support became a lifeline for me. Some days later, I received the news that my ex-boyfriend had turned himself in. It became safe to come home again. I am eternally grateful for the love and hospitality they showed me. God bless them for keeping a girl safe at a troubled time and feeding her rum-raisin ice cream.

It was a time to grow up fast. By now it was January 1994 and I was starting the new year with my first doctor visit. A quick test at the clinic confirmed my pregnancy and this time the news was not so shocking. Weighing in at just over 90 pounds, there was a major concern for how low my weight was. It was so hard to eat and keep food down. Putting on the pounds was going to take extra work. Even though taking care of my own health was not important to me before, it suddenly mattered. How I lived would directly affect my baby. My eyes got big when I saw the size of the prenatal vitamins. I wondered how I would swallow one and keep it down. That did not stop me because I was determined to do whatever it took.

It was at the local clinic that I heard my baby's heartbeat for the first time. The sound was unforgettable, and I was in awe. Hope now had a sound. This was really happening! To the best of my ability, I did everything the doctors instructed me to do.

Now focused, I returned to school full time and returned to work at the library part time. The benefit here, is that at the library I had access to books and information on whatever I wanted to know about. On slow nights, I would shelf books, then look over books that caught my attention. It was there that I discovered a book about dating violence for teens titled <u>In Love and In Danger</u>. I learned about the red flags of an abusive dating relationship like being afraid to disagree, being hit or shoved, and being secretive among other things. This book showed me I was not alone. It gave me information that changed my life!

I also came back just in time to start my second and final semester of high school. My goal was to graduate on time with my class. My life's experiences became the subject of some of my required English writing assignments. It also became a form of soul searching and helped me to deal with what I had been through. The research that I did for a paper on teen pregnancy showed me that I was not alone. I found this kind of writing to be healing for me. Over the years, journal writing has been an essential way to sort through my feelings. As I look back on things I have written, I can see growth and reflect on the choices I have made. It has proven to be a great tool to help me learn about myself.

> "Strength does not always roar, sometimes it shows up like quiet determination."

At first, only a few of my closest friends knew about my pregnancy. On my first day back, I remember walking into the building with my friends. We were among a sea of students that had just gotten off the bus. "Can they look at me and tell?" I wondered. Now I was "that girl". Commonly, pregnant women are told that they are "glowing" because of how well they look. Then there was me, a skinny girl with braces and a secret weighing on my shoulders. I wouldn't really call that glowing. Little by little people started to find out. I had to face all kinds of reactions. The usual questions were about how my mom felt or how my baby's father felt. It was not until my guidance counselor asked me how I felt that I realized no one had asked me that before. I was faced with dealing with my own feelings again. How did I feel? Happy, nervous, scared, hopeful, uncertain...With so many feelings crashing over me, surprisingly I found a quiet strength arising in me as well.

Around that time, a detective made a home visit to ask about a dispute that my mom had with our neighbor. He made the visit personally because he knew my ex-boyfriend and realized our connection to him. The detective eventually changed the conversation over to my baby's father. I explained some of our story and the situation I was in. Without hesitation, he encouraged me to terminate my pregnancy.

> "As a mother, you are your baby's first protector."

"You'll be tied to this guy forever," he advised. I found no compassion in his words and I was stunned. I do not remember saying anything out loud. It was more like silent rage. Didn't he know, that risk was a small price to pay? My outrage at those words affirmed my motherhood. I can't explain how, but that silent rage turned into this feeling that somehow, I was going to make it. Strength does not always roar, sometimes it shows up like quiet determination.

What if I was insecure or unsure of my decision to keep my baby? What if his suggestion was the last straw that sent me to the abortion clinic? Words have power.

Even though my mom never talked to me about abortion, in the core of my being I knew that it was wrong. Being raised by a single mother, I saw my mom sacrifice for me. This was my example. My upbringing was not a traditional one or even ideal, but it was full of bravery. The message to me was clear. Mothers care and sacrifice for their children.

If you are still in the process of deciding what to do, let's take it slow right now. Hear my heart. I know you are scared. Decisions are being made that will affect the rest of your life. They will impact your baby's father and each of your families. No matter how rough your situation may be, you are not in this alone. Take a moment to look up and look around. There are people out there willing to help you and your baby. Some will surprise you in the best way. My mom surprised me when she welcomed be back home. Her love brought me back to life when I was at my weakest. My friends' support encouraged me when I thought I didn't deserve it. Even if you don't see how you could keep your baby, please understand that an abortion will cause your heart double the pain. The loss of a child is agony and knowing the loss was your choice will cause your heart suffering unlike any other. This baby's life matters and so does yours. Your heart matters. Every tear matters. The pain and failed expectations, it all matters. This baby inside of you, is a person with a heartbeat and a purpose of their own. They are just smaller than you and me. As a mother, you are your baby's first protector. If you got pregnant as the result of a traumatic experience, I am so sorry. I imagine this makes it an especially difficult time. Please do what you can to seek help for yourself. When you do an online search for "crisis pregnancy center" I believe you will find more help than you thought was available. If you are leaning more towards an abortion, I ask that you please consider your child's innocent life and the possibility of giving another family hope through adoption. Keep in mind, that there are women out there experiencing a different kind of pain. The kind that comes from wanting a child but not being able to have one.

A few years after high school, I had a close friend that chose to have an abortion. She came home, curled up in a corner and could not stop shaking. The joy that I was used to seeing in her eyes was gone. I did not recognize her, she was a wreck. My friend was heartbroken. Heavy with guilt and shame, it did not take long before she became pregnant again. This time she kept the baby. I can't help but to wonder if that time was on purpose, to comfort her broken heart.

I believe that only God is the giver of life, and that every life has purpose and value. Somewhere deep inside I think we know that. I have never met a woman that was glad she had an abortion. Instead, I have found that women carry the secret around like an invisible mark of shame. I do not believe the choice to have an abortion is an easy one. I also believe that women who have not had to make such a decision, do not have a clear understanding how conflicting it is.

If you have had an abortion in the past I want to stop right here for you.

I am so sorry for your loss. I imagine you must have been so afraid. This is not how it was supposed to be, and I hurt with you. Even if you do not believe it, you are forgivable, and you are lovable. There is there is grace to wash out the darkest parts of your life. I want you to know there is help for you. Hope exists and is available to everyone, even you. Especially you. There is a God that loves you and understands your pain. He knows that working through the mess and the chaos is worth it, if it means getting to you. He knows that you are worth it. If you need to cry, then cry. If you need to scream, then scream. Denying the pain is an option, but then how can you heal? Consider this:

> "The LORD is close to the brokenhearted
> and saves those who are crushed in spirit."
> Psalm 34:18

Have you ever seen a small child out in public having a tantrum and causing destruction? He might get hurt in the process and throw another fit? Even when the parent is there to bring comfort, the child might refuse the help because he is so upset.

Please, do not choose to be like that child. Please do not turn away because you feel unworthy of love and forgiveness. The Bible describes God as a Good Father that knows how much you hurt. He cannot be compared to the father that you have known on this earth, no matter how good or bad he was. God is perfectly good. He knows the secrets of your heart and is big enough to handle everything you want to say…or scream.

I am fully aware that you may be reading this and not even believe in God. Maybe so much has happened to you that you doubt or reject the idea of God all together. That is your right. All I ask is that you listen and examine what I am saying for yourself. I tell you these things because I do believe in God. I have also come to believe that healing is possible regardless of how bad the situation is. Would you consider hearing me out all the way?

During my pregnancy, I started to receive collect phone calls from my baby's father who was in jail. Every choice to accept or reject a call was a choice that was affecting my future. Slowly, I returned to the relationship, but I was starting over from an emotionally stronger place. Phone calls turned into Saturday field trips to the local jail. This was an all-day commitment, made up of multiple bus rides and hours of waiting.

I had joined a secret club of mostly women who cared for someone that was locked-up. Membership was expensive, and the rewards were small. When we were together, we barely made eye-contact, but we were aware of each other's presence. Outside the jail, no one wants to admit they are members of this club. When I saw someone on the outside I was somewhat excited because I thought, "Hey look, they are a real person with a normal life too, just like me." We might have shared a quick glance, but that was it.

As a visitor at a correctional facility, there are several hoops to jump through to see an inmate. You must keep a mental list of what to make sure you bring, like your ID or what not to bring, like anything that would set off a metal detector. While I waited patiently in the waiting area, I mentally played this game of who was going to make it through and who would be turned away. Temporary relief only came for us when we encountered the faces of the ones we came to see.

It seemed that the need to be loved by my baby's father was stronger than the memory of what he put me through. Life behind bars put limits on our relationship. This gave me the freedom to come and go as I pleased. This time of separation gave me time to breathe and grow as a person. Still, through his phone calls he drilled me with questions about where I had gone and who I had been with. Based on my previous reading, I could recognize this as a red flag. Whoever made the observation that "knowledge is power" was right!

As I began to taste more peace and freedom, I became less tolerant of his behavior. I learned that I had a larger support system than I thought. There was my mom, my friends, the school counselor, community organizations, the staff at the clinic and my teachers. Looking at it this way, no single mom is ever truly alone.

As the months went by, my body started to visibly change. I also developed a strange skin sensitivity. No one else could see it but I could feel it. Everything I put on itched. I had to wear all my clothes inside out, down to my underwear, in order to avoid the seam. There were many more doctor visits, tests and ongoing blood work. A few tests were scary even though they were routine. After the doctor gets done explaining the risks, it is easy to think the worst. That made the waiting game torture. Worrying my mom was the last thing I wanted, I had already put her through so much. It was hard to share those moments. My close friends were the bomb. I felt that I had not been such a great friend to them by leaving but their friendship stayed true. Being around them gave me a sense of normalcy. They listened and kept me laughing. They did the best they could even when they didn't know what I was going through firsthand.

There were good days and bad days. A good day was the time I first felt my baby move inside me. I will never forget I was sitting crisscrossed on my sofa in my living room watching television. Suddenly, like a little fish come alive, I felt him wiggling around. What an amazing feeling! My little one was making himself known to me in a whole new way. I had felt so connected to my baby before, it felt like this was his way of responding.

I was in awe over my first sonogram. To anyone else, the image might have looked like a black and white snapshot of an alien, but not to me. People typically asked me if I wanted to know the sex of my baby. Honestly, I love surprises and I did not want to know. Late in my pregnancy something out of the ordinary happened. One night, I had a dream of a little boy in light blue pajamas. He was standing with his hands on a floor mirror much bigger than he was. With a head full of dark hair, a round little tan face and big dark-brown eyes, he looked over at me as he banged on the glass. My heart was completely captured. I know it may sound wild, but this turned out to be a true glimpse of what my son would look like almost one year later.

The end of my senior year came quickly. My friends were excited about the senior class trip and the prom. My excitement and attention were set in another direction. My baby bump was growing, and my clothes were shrinking. Since I was so petite, from the back I still looked like just one of the girls. Once I turned around, however, it was obvious that I was very pregnant. There were several senior year events that took place, but my choices were limited. I was able to make it to a special dinner for graduating seniors. That meant the fun of getting dressed up, putting make-up on and being with my friends for the night. We had a great time reminiscing and laughing through the picture slideshow. It was just enough to make me feel like just another teenager again.

Little by little, the relationship with my mom improved. We had our rocky moments because I was still 17 and loaded with extra hormones. It must have been hard on her. Until my early teens my mom worked mostly two jobs. A few times she even worked three jobs. With all the time away she spent working, I had formed my own style of independence. She stopped working due to arthritis a few years earlier, which meant she was home more. My mom wanted to lay down the law, but by then it felt like she was too late. By then, I had convinced myself that she had no right to tell me what to do. I would rebel against her requests and she would fight back with the silent treatment. As an adult I have learned that my core fear is disconnection from people I love, so you can imagine what that did to me. It was a difficult time for us. Still, as much as I fought to be independent, I was starting to see how much I needed her.

On the day of my high school graduation I was about seven months pregnant. It did not matter to me how I looked in front of the crowd. I simply wobbled up to the platform and waited for my name to be called to receive my diploma. I had made it! What a great sense of accomplishment for me and a proud moment for us all. You must understand, my mom had to drop out of school at a young age. There was this sense that I was not just graduating for me but for my family - the one I had and the one yet to be. I had earned so much more than my diploma that day.

You are not alone!

There are numerous decisions to be made and the demands are coming at you fast. Remember you are not alone. The people that surround you may not know exactly how you feel and that is okay. If they are supportive do not turn them away.

Make a list of the support system that you have access to. You may find you have more than you thought (parents, baby's father, friends, extended family, counselors, teachers, doctors, nurses, etc.)

Being grateful is a small thing that can make a huge difference. Can you name at least three things that you are grateful for right now?

3

This is My Son

After graduation, I had two months to think and plan. This was the time to focus on what preparations had to be made within my small budget. I took great pride in picking out my baby's clothes. At this point, I still had no crib and no car seat. At a local thrift store, I found exactly the crib I needed. Through my searching, I also found a local non-profit organization that would lend me a car seat for a few months. With humble beginnings, things started to come together. Although I did not have a driver's license or even a learner's permit, that was no problem most of the time. As New Yorkers, we were used to using public transportation to get around. We also had a family friend that was kind enough to help us out when we needed a ride.

We did not have the newest and best of everything, but my heart was content. Life was about to change in the most beautiful way, I was going to be a mother. Not really having been much of a clean freak before, I unexpectedly had this boost of energy and focus to wash all the baby clothes I had. I scrubbed the crib like a mad woman. I rearranged my room and fit in the new crib. Apparently, this overwhelming urge has a name. It is called nesting.

Closer to my due date I had a second sonogram. I saw the cutest image of my baby yawning. It was adorable! The idea of having a baby to care for was becoming more real every day. With only some minor health issues, I was more of a homebody than ever. Some nights I laid down to sleep and my baby thought the party was just getting started. He would kick non-stop, but I loved every moment.

One summer morning I woke up with a stomach ache. It was so early that it was still dark. Here's the deal. When you are pregnant and feeling discomfort, you mentally run down the list. Is it gas? Am I hungry? Do I have to go to the bathroom?

I decided on having an ice-cream pop to soothe me while I figured it out. My stomach ache went away but then it came back. Again. And again. After a few more times of this discomfort coming and going I got the bright idea to keep my eye on the clock. It was consistently every 5-7 minutes apart.

This was NOT a stomach ache. These were contractions! It was two weeks before my due date and the pains were not sharp. It was more a sensation of cramping and back discomfort, so I did not think it was labor. I jumped into full panic mode and I started thinking, "I need a shower! I need clean clothes! I need umm...the hospital! I need to get to the hospital!" After a painful attempt at a quick shower, an ambulance came for me around 9 o'clock in the morning. It felt like the bumpiest ride ever! That did not help my contractions. When the nurse checked me out I thought for sure it was a false alarm. I would be back home in no time, right? After all, it was a couple of weeks before my due date. Then I heard the words that rocked my world in an instant, "You're going to have this baby today!" You can imagine the look on my face.

That summer morning had started cozy and quietly in my own bed and was suddenly exploding with action. There were nurses and doctors buzzing all around me. When my nurse was called away I heard her refuse. She snapped back, "No, Blanca is my patient." Wow. It was so encouraging to hear that someone cared that much. I found myself in the middle of the chaos between papers that needed to be signed and decisions that demanded my attention. A staff person asked that if a C-section needed to be done, would I want to be asleep or awake? Uh, asleep? Surely, it did not matter anyway, because I was going to have my baby naturally.

Having my mom there was comforting. It was hectic to have one person checking on my blood pressure, a second asking me a series of medical questions and the doctor at the foot of my bed about to break my water. It all happened so fast! There wasn't even time to feel embarrassed at all the different people examining my body. During labor, the doctor could see that my baby was in fetal distress. In other words, the heartbeat monitor was warning us that something was not right. The idea of a natural childbirth flew right out the window, and I was headed for an emergency C-section.

> "The next time I woke up I was officially a little person's mom."

I was rushed away to the surgery room without my mom. With her limited English and the chaos of everything, she must have been so scared. In the blink of an eye, this shy, quiet girl was being stripped naked in a room full of people. There was no time to feel ashamed. I was moved to the operating table and my belly was wiped down with betadine. I felt a warm blanket placed over me and my arms were strapped down. An oxygen mask was placed over my mouth, and I was moments away from a life changing deep sleep. The nurse softly asked me to count down starting from ten. "10, 9, 8..." That is all I remember.

The next time I woke up I was officially a little person's mom. Not only had a child been born that day, a new me was birthed, too. There was a baby, a birth certificate, and a new page in our family's story.

I regained consciousness even before I could open my eyes. Something was strangely different in my body where my baby bump had been. Still groggy, I turned and saw my mom next to me. She told me what I already knew, "It's a boy," she said softly in Spanish. I was so pleased, and my heart was filled with love before I even laid eyes on him. She explained that from the next room she heard his cry when they took him out. What a special moment that must have been for her.

Shortly after, I learned that my precious little boy was having trouble feeding. The hospital informed me that they would be transferring him to another one better equipped to treat him. I was still coming down from the anesthesia, but I do have a memory of having him by my bedside for a moment. When I reached over to see him, I knew we would soon be separated. There was sadness in knowing I could not have him close to me. I had come to the hospital to have my baby and I had planned on leaving with him but that was not possible anymore. A feeling of peace came in knowing they would provide the special care that he needed. I quickly came to terms with the fact that the hospital and I wanted the same thing. We both wanted my baby to get better and that kept my worries under control. I had learned how healthy and important a mother's breast milk was, so I agreed to let the nurses set me up to pump my own. It seemed unfair and unnatural to attach a machine to my boob in the place of my baby. It was a reminder that I was missing out on having him close to me. The hospital would transport the milk to where he was, and it gave me a sense of accomplishment.

"He gave me hope again, and inspired me to be a better person."

My son's entrance into this world was unplanned and now I could not make a plan without him. Everything would become about him and what he needed. This little seed of hope now had a presence on this side of eternity and I became protective right away. When the time came for his birth certificate, I named him Ricky, after his father. That is what we had decided on earlier when things were well, and I kept my word. They could share the name, but I was determined to make sure he would know a different life. The truth is, no matter who we were as parents and what we had done, this was a brand new little person. A clean slate.

In the hospital, my mom stayed with me most of the time and she demonstrated such dedication. She made sure I was eating and well cared for. Whenever I woke up she was there. I had my own baby to care for but that did not change the fact that I was her baby first. We spent the time talking, sleeping and laughing. Anything that required stomach muscles was so painful. Knowing that I should not laugh, made everything so much funnier! Once, I heard someone say that life was like a wheel and laughter was the grease that kept it going smoothly. Considering the situation, laughter was just what we needed.

During one of her visits, my mom brought me a letter from my baby's father. He had no way of knowing what was going on. He didn't know that I was laid up in a hospital bed and that there were problems during my labor. In the letter, he wrote that he hadn't heard from me in a while and asked if I could send him money for a pair of sneakers. "Are you kidding me?!" I thought. I am a kind person, but that was not my problem homeboy. Especially not on this day.

When I was released from the hospital, my main goal was to see Ricky. My friends were kind and made the trip to go see him after he was transferred. Since they did not drive they had to rely on their parents. I asked one friend to check on Ricky when I couldn't make it. She told me later that she showed up and was able to see him only after pretending to be my sister. That meant so much to me! My mom and I had to have a family friend give us a ride whenever we went to see him. Our visits were short, and took every ounce of energy I had. I remember during our first visit I reached my hand into the incubator to gently rubbed his little back. It was a bit hairy and felt like peach fuzz. I thought, "Yup, that's my baby." He was so small, his diaper looked like it was about to swallow him whole. After seeing how much he was cared for, between the nurses and the machines, it put me at ease. The nurses called him "peanut" because he was so small. At birth, Ricky was only five pounds and 17 1/2 inches. He is so big now, if you saw him today you would never have guessed he started out so small. The NICU (neonatal intensive care unit) gave me a handmade knitted blanket. It was made by volunteers for babies that stayed there. This act of kindness mattered to me and I have kept that blanket after all these years. There is no such thing as a small good deed.

Almost two weeks later, Ricky had gained enough weight to come home. I was so excited to receive the news that I locked myself out of my apartment. Then, I was so anxious to get to the hospital that I realized half way there, that I had forgotten my ID. Another setback, really? Was I being pranked? I was so eager to bring him home and yet, it felt as if someone had hit the slow-motion button on my life! I finally made it to the hospital with the smallest outfit I could find. It was still too big for him, he could only fill it up half way. As I placed him into the car seat he nearly disappeared into it as well. That night we picked up Chinese take-out to celebrate and spent hours taking turns to hold him.

I could not wait to take him out in public and present him to the world. I still remember the first time someone asked me who he was. I was glad to speak up and say confidently, "This is my son." I could not stop smiling. I was introducing a little piece of heaven that had invaded my plans in the best way. Having Ricky made me want to be a good mother. He gave me hope again, and inspired me to be a better person. It felt as though God was entrusting me with one of His treasures and I was so fired up to rise to the occasion.

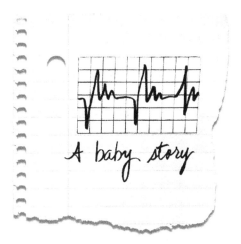

Everyone's delivery story is different. Each story takes turns that are funny, scary and overall unforgettable. When the time comes, take a moment to describe your experience and celebrate your baby's birth day.

What details do you remember?

Who was there?

What was it like when you saw your baby for the first time?

4

A Brave New Me

Every day I worked at getting used to my new routine. I loved the feeling of resting Ricky on my chest and gently rubbing his back. At that age babies are so warm and squishy, perfect for snuggling. Sometimes, I would hold him in my lap and just stare. Who did he look like more, I wondered? He had a full head of spikey hair, dark and soft like me. Every time I looked at him, I found that I was looking at my own reflection. I was amazed. Looking into his beautiful dark brown eyes I could not help but make silent promises. There was a longing in me for him to get what I didn't get as a child.

Every 24 hours there was a rotating schedule of feedings, burping, changing diapers, cleaning spit ups and sleeping. There was nothing glamorous about it. Some late nights I would give him a bottle and doze off halfway through. I would wake up startled only to find I had the bottle pressed against his cheek. He then had a trail of formula running down his face to his neck and onesie. Taking naps were not just for Ricky, they became a lifesaver for me as well. Lack of sleep and proper rest can make you super cranky and behave in ways that you normally would not. In the beginning, bath time was hard for me. I thought he was so fragile that he would fall apart in my hands if I moved him around too much or gave him a gentle scrub. The hospital where Ricky spend his first two weeks had a program for young moms like me. The staff was great. It was a place to receive care for myself, not just my baby. They encouraged me to sing to my baby, read to him and taught me how to swaddle him. Thankfully, I got past some of my fears. After watching how the nurses handled him I realized he was not going to fall apart. They helped to build my confidence and Ricky eventually received a decent bath.

My mom was also huge help. She was my right hand. It was through Ricky, that I discovered a whole new side of her. I saw a softer side, a more playful side. Ricky also became a buffer to her silent treatments. For the sake of Ricky, we needed to communicate. We could not afford to punish each other with silence. Just as I had found a whole new level of love, so did she. It was obvious. She was a proud grandmother. My mom once told me that she did not think she would live long enough to see grandchildren. I got used to seeing her light up when she told people, "Es my grandson," with her broken English. It still makes me smile.

"Even though I was not in college like my friends, motherhood had enrolled me in a school of its own."

Spending time with my friends was possible but not nearly as often as before. Getting a grip on my new life was my focus. I was learning a new normal. Through motherhood I was discovering a brand new me. I took Ricky out for walks and loved for people to meet him. He was an adorable baby and naturally drew attention. I lost track of the times I heard people say, "Is that your little brother?" It was in those moments that I was reminded of my status as a teen mom and not a typical mom.

Etched in my memory is a baby-sitting job my mom took about three years earlier. One day the baby cried so much that eventually I was the one crying. So much effort was put into trying to comfort this baby, but he was not having it. During my pregnancy, I remembered this experience and it made me worry. How would I handle my own baby if I could not get him to stop crying? Would I freak out? Would I be the one to end up crying?

It turns out, the cry of my own child was not scary to me at all. Frustrating at times, but not scary. Somehow, I understood that his crying did not mean I was a bad mom. Since he could not speak, it was his way of communicating he was hungry, sleepy, had a dirty diaper or was in pain. Once when Ricky was about nine months old, he cried for what seemed like hours. We tried all kinds of things. I finally called a co-worker who had two small children of her own. She rushed over like a super hero with a small bottle in hand. With one or two drops, instantaneously Ricky stopped crying. What. The. Heck. You might be wondering what the mystery pain causing all the chaos was about? Good ol' fashion gas. It was gas, people! I had no clue.

Then there was the time when Ricky seemed to be feverish all the time when he first came home. Worry would set in when I would touch his red little cheeks and feel how hot he was. I took him to the doctor as soon as they would see me. Was it serious? Nope, not a life-threatening disease at all. It turns out I should not have bundled up my summer baby like I was preparing him for a winter blizzard. The doctor told me, to dress him like I would dress myself. "If you are cold, he will probably be cold. If you are warm, chances are he will be too," he explained. Not sure where I got the idea from, but I thought that my baby needed to be extra bundled up all the time. Ok doc, no more Eskimo baby fashion.

Being a mom is scary at any age. These are just a few of the many lessons I learned the hard way. Even though I was not in college like my friends, motherhood had enrolled me in a school of its own.

Learning never ends. My son is an adult now, and I am still learning how to be the mom he needs me to be. The best thing I did when I did not know what to do was to reach out for help.

Graduating from high school meant one major thing was out of the way. College was not on my radar, and I had no stable job in sight. After I gave birth, I could stay home for a few months and catch my breath. This time to enjoy my new baby was a special gift, and allowed time for bonding. It also gave me time to think of what I would do next. When the time came I did what I had learned in school. I put together a resume and searched for work. My efforts landed me a position as a receptionist in an insurance agency, five towns away. It was a long bus ride away, but it meant we could have private health insurance. I was thankful for the government assistance I had received up to that point, but I was tired of going to clinics and waiting for long periods of time. Tired of meeting new doctors at almost every visit. This new opportunity afforded us the ability to see a doctor that would be our own family doctor. A doctor that would remember my baby and me each time we went.

While I was working, my mom was a great support in caring for Ricky. It was not easy though. My mom had one way of doing things and I had another. While this became a source of frustration, overall I had few reasons to complain. She was also learning that there was a new side of me to appreciate. A more responsible side of me began to emerge. With Ricky as our common goal, we did our best to make it work.

You might be wondering where my baby's father was in all this? Our relationship was falling apart. Again. This time with less drama because he was not around. He had been transferred from a local jail to a state prison and I was growing used to his absence. It meant more peace in my life. When he was away, there were no crazy cycles in the picture. Growing up there is a phrase my mom would say. "Es mejor estar sola que mal acompañada." It means, it is better to be alone than in bad company. I began to understand exactly what she meant.

> "I took his abuse in the past, but my thinking had changed."

Ricky was probably two or three months old when his father held him for the first time. He came to see us after his release on parole. This new father smiled big and I could see he was in awe. Truthfully, it was heartwarming. "Maybe, this would turn into a wakeup call for him like it was for me," I thought. "Maybe, now our relationship had a serious chance." Can you tell I still wanted things to work out? Between the library and school, I had done plenty of reading and preparing over the last several months. It was changing me and what I wanted in life. I had a better idea of what a healthy relationship was and was not.

I took his abuse in the past, but my thinking had changed. I could not bear the thought of exposing my son to the same thing. I wanted more for Ricky. It's no way for a child to live. Considering the circumstances, we allowed him to live with the three of us for a short time. The stress of being tight on money, carrying unresolved anger and his dependence on alcohol proved to be too much for him. It was not long before my baby's father fell into old patterns. Our arguments kept escalating, and so did the anxiety.

He came to my home drunk one day at 4am. I told him if he did not leave I would throw out his clothes and he threatened to kill me. His response may sound extreme, but if we take a closer look at the situation it was not about clothes. My empowerment meant one thing: he was losing control over me.

A few weeks later we had another incident that put me over the edge and sent me searching for how to file for an order of protection. During an argument, I was trying to prevent him from getting through the front door. I could smell the very familiar scent of alcohol on him. By then it had become a warning of things to come. He managed to grab me and pull me away from the door. In the process my foot was hurt, and I knew it was only a matter of time before it was more than just my foot. Honestly, I don't remember how that night ended. Whatever happened, it was enough to push me to take action. Ricky was five months old when I filed and was granted a temporary order of protection against his father. Additionally, I filed a petition for full legal custody of our son. After a few court dates my petition was granted. I imagine it would have been hard to fight my request from a jail cell.

That may sound cold, but taking that step was hard for me to do. It was difficult because I still loved him and had hope that he was capable of change. I was being pulled between the need to protect my family, and the guilt of letting go of the dream of having a complete family. My decision meant I was cutting him off from his support system. Hope was being restored in so many different areas of my life because of this amazing baby. I thought he would step up his game, but sadly, I was disappointed. I used to think of grieving as the suffering that a person goes through when their loved one dies. Now I believe that it is possible, and perhaps necessary, to grieve when a dream dies. The dream of the three of us as a family was gone.

"When we forgive, that means the one who hurt us does not owe us anything."

I did not walk alone in this process. Thankfully, a local organization set me up with an advocate. She was a young woman who went with me to the court for support and explained each step of the process. In moments of weakness it tore my heart to stick to my decision. I remember at one of the court appointments seeing my baby's father in handcuffs and being escorted by an officer into the courtroom. I tried so hard to read his face. Should I make eye contact or not? It was tormenting. This was the first time I had ever been in a courtroom and it was intimidating. We stood before the judge on opposite sides and even then, I questioned whether this was the right thing to do.

It was times like these that I felt horrible to keep him away when he wanted to be with us. It was too late though. My eyes were opened. Through this experience I had done some growing up and discovered a brave new me. The separation was not part of my original plan. I came to understand it was the result of the choices he had made. His own decisions had created the gap between us.

Outside of us, my baby's father had no family and no support system close by. Since we could no longer be that for him, he started to crumble under the pressures of life. His acquaintances were drinking buddies and he had trouble getting a job. That combination was not good for him or us. The order of protection violated his parole, and it sent him back to prison to finish his time. After his release, he moved down south to be with family.

With time and distance working against us, our communication became less frequent. A major decision that helped me to heal was the choice to forgive. I was able to do respond this way because it is the way my mom had responded to me. The lesson here is that, I could make this person a prisoner of my bitterness or set him free. Taking into consideration the way he was raised and the hell he went through way before he met me, I chose to forgive my baby's father. I chose to believe he did the best he could with what he knew at the time. Looking back through the years, I see that this perspective allowed me to be healthy enough to make better choices for myself.

I purposed in my heart never to speak negatively about him to my son. I knew that if I did, I would only be crushing a part of who my son is. Keeping secrets were not an option either. Over the years, I did my best to give Ricky information that was appropriate for his age. He knew the truth and was always allowed to ask questions.

A word about forgiveness. When we forgive, that means the one who hurt us does not owe us anything. It is like cancelling a financial debt. Let's say someone owes you money. You think of the $20 they owe you every time you see them or think of them. You can get angry when they show up with a mani/pedi, knowing full well they owe you money. Then one day you realize you must move on. You decide it's not worth the trouble to stress over what they owe you. As an act of mercy, you choose to let it go and no longer hold the debt against the person. Now when you think of that person, you think of them as a person and not what they owe you. That is what forgiveness is like.

Our forgiveness cancels out anything we believe we are owed. When I say, "I forgive," but I am still waiting for that person to pay me back for the wrong they did me, then I have not forgiven in the truest sense of the word. It is dangerous to wait for a person to be sorry enough or worthy enough to be forgiven. Mark my words, unforgiveness will lead to bitterness. As time goes on, bitterness starts to touch other relationships and damage them. It begins to separate us from people that love us and want to help.

There was a powerful lesson that I didn't expect to learn from my mom. After hurting her by running away and betraying her trust, my mom forgave me. She made the choice for us to have a fresh start. The issue was not about me "earning" forgiveness, but rather that she considered that I was worthy of forgiving. She held the key.

Everyone has the potential of being forgiven and offering forgiveness. Everyone. Right now, in your mind, you may be going through a list and think "Nope, not this person." Yes, that person. You hold the key.

Mirror, mirror

Motherhood changes every woman. It doesn't matter if our pregnancy was planned or not. We begin to discover things about ourselves that we did not know was there. What we see when we look in the mirror is our choice.

Can you name at least three positive things you like about yourself?

What about your baby's father?

What has been your hardest decision so far?

5

Growing Up

There were plenty of milestones and reasons to celebrate in those first few years:

- first tooth
- first steps
- first words
- first vaccine shots
- first haircut
- first birthday

Watching Ricky roll over for the first time was adorable. Realizing it meant he might roll of the bed was scary. Taking him to his first doctor visit was exciting. Watching him scream after three seconds of frozen silence as he got his first vaccine shots was terrifying. Even though he was the one having a bunch of "firsts" we were all experiencing them together. Everyone around him was trying to coach him into his first word. Quite naturally every mother wants their baby's first word to be "mama" and every father wants it to be "dada". Ricky's first word was cookie. I have a sweet tooth myself, so I guess I can't blame him! On his first birthday, just a handful of my friends came over to my home to celebrate with us. It was intimate and sweet. Surviving the first year with my sanity intact was cause for celebration too!

"Everyday was filled with teachable moments."

Motherhood kept surprising me. It continued to pull out of me someone I never imagined myself to be. Love was becoming a state of being, not just a feeling. I found myself singing silly songs and telling stories with sound effects. Who cares what I looked like if I was making Ricky happy, right? Anything to see him smile. When I found a sound that made him giggle, of course, I had to put it on repeat to make him laugh over and over. What if we did that for ourselves? Instead of replaying bad things, what if we focused on something innocent and good to repeat for the sheer enjoyment of it? Laughter is good for the soul, remember that. When Buddy the Elf insisted, "Smiling is my favorite!" he was onto something big.

Children have a natural way of calling out the innocence and fun in us. Ricky was no different. We played "patty cakes" and celebrated little victories like waving goodbye or doing a high-five. Going for walks downtown or taking our old bread to feed the ducks by the water became part of our little adventures.

With work and school taking so much of my time, I did my best to enjoy our time together. Our outings also had to fit our budget. Every single parent must learn how to make their dollars stretch. Several times we ended up at the petting zoo to feed the goats or took trips to the library for story time.

This sounds picture-perfect and stress-free, right? Do not be fooled, I messed up too. Like the time Ricky slipped out of his baby carrier and onto the wooden floor. I had not secured him in because I was only moving him just a few feet across the room and barely lifted the carrier off the floor. I felt horrible. I am sure my heart stopped for about five seconds, but he was fine.

Then, there was the time that we were at a Christmas parade and Ricky needed to go to the bathroom. He was new at potty-training and I had to get him to a bathroom, pronto! We went to a clothing store and made it just in time. I was in such a rush to get back to the parade, that I did not realize that his pants had not been pulled up. I was practically dragging him through the store at high speed when we realized his pants were around his ankles. Thankfully his winter coat was long enough to cover him up. Who does that? Ugh, sorry Ricky.

Everyday was filled with teachable moments. Not just for Ricky, for you me too! There is this one trip we took to the park that I remember clearly because I walked away with a deep revelation. There were not many others there, but I do remember a certain woman and her child. This woman was so careful with her child, too careful almost. At every turn the mother was right there warning her child not to get hurt. With her sounds and her body language she was letting her child know how scared she was. I found myself being sad for that little child who had no space to learn.

Ricky was old enough to climb the jungle gym and I decided to stay within a few feet. I wanted to give him space and let him discover the trickiness of climbing this jungle gym. Even when he got stuck, I waited and watched. It was when he asked for help or I saw the fear in his eyes that I came over to his rescue. Even though he would have the potential of a minor bump or bruise, I let him figure out how to climb up and climb down without much instruction. When he learned how to get unstuck, I would celebrate him. When he would try and fail, I would cheer him for trying. That day I made a decision. I wanted him to understand early on, that pain is a part of life, but it would not be the end of the world. When we give space for our children to make mistakes in a controlled setting, we honor the learning process.

People get teased about being a control freak. Even the most low-key, chill-kind-of-person like me, struggles with issues of control. This gets challenged in motherhood with great intensity.

> "Maybe, motherhood is about us growing up, too."

When your child is newly born, this is probably the most control you will ever have over them. What they eat, what they wear, and who they are with, are just a few decisions of a much longer list of things you can control. Once they start walking you have less control over the things they walk into, such as a busy parking lot. As much as you obsess over holding your child's hand, you will probably have a parking lot scare at least once in your life. When they start talking, you will soon realize how quickly they can say something in public that will leave you completely embarrassed with no warning.

These become teachable moments. They become important because you won't always be there. You want to make sure that you have given them enough training over time that they will carry the lessons with them throughout their life. Lessons on sharing, kindness, sticking up for yourself and manners just to name a few. Warning: this is not just a one-time deal.

Think of it this way. Getting it wrong will be natural for them because they just don't know. It is our job as parents to teach and train them. Many times, you will be going over the same lessons over and over again. That sounds boring but that's what training is, right? In sports, these repetitive actions are called drills. Something you do continuously, so that when it is game time, you are as prepared as possible. No matter how amazing a player is, she still must do the same drills as the team player that has the least skills. There is no need to be mad about repeating yourself, embrace it as a part of your new life as a mom.

As children become toddlers, you will notice a resistance. Having my son tell me "I do it!" when it is clear he cannot tie his shoes, is normal. It is not so much about them being mean, rather they are in the process of exercising a sense of independence. Some children are more verbal about this than others. It is in our best interest not to take this personal. We are their first teacher. If we are impatient, the chances that they will be too, is much higher. If we exercise patience, then we model for them how it is done.

Remember mama bear, motherhood is the process of letting go and handing over control. Loving your children? Yes. Preparing your children? Absolutely. And letting go, eventually. Let's be real, it is bittersweet. Actually, it must be both. When they are little you will let go of the responsibility to tie their shoes and ask them to handle it. When they are a teenager (yikes), you will let go of driving them places and they will be in control of driving themselves. My son is an adult now and I am telling you – letting go never ends.

There is a myth floating around out there. "It gets easier when they get older." Simply not true. Motherhood and parenting has seasons. Every time a season changes you will trade in one set of challenges in for another. That also means a fresh new set of opportunities to grow and make memories.

For every stage, the process of letting go looks different. Maybe, motherhood is about us growing up, too. This is a lesson I hope you take from me. Honestly, looking back I wish I was much more patient and not as quick to lose my temper. Our little ones have real feelings that can get hurt if we do not get ourselves under control. If we do lose our cool, we need to be quick to recognize it and ask for forgiveness.

You may have grown up with parenting that goes like this. "I am the parent and I should be in control. You, the child, should let me control you because I love you and I know what is best for you." At some point the story takes a turn and the parent does not understand that their child is growing up. What a parent wants to express but does not know how is, "I know I am losing control over you. I am scared. I just don't know how to let go." Instead it may look like yelling, fear and stricter control, even abuse.

There was a time when Ricky would climb out of his crib and come find me. He would wake up much earlier than I was ready for and fall asleep again in my bed. It was cute for a little while, but I didn't want him to form a bad habit. For every bad habit I allowed I would have to work hard to correct later. I thought it might be time to graduate him from a crib to a toddler bed. I was so excited because this was going to be another "first" for us.

Overall, once Ricky fell sleep, he did a fairly good job at staying that way through the night. After he learned to get out of his crib it became difficult to trust that he would stay there. I bought a new bed, and picked out the cutest Mickey Mouse bed set I could find. Ricky was amused by the idea but when that first night for bed time came around he was not having it. He cried. I firmly let him know it was bed time and he had to stay. He cried some more and this time louder. To be real, I do not remember how he finally fell asleep that night. I am guessing I gave up and let him fall asleep in my bed. I vaguely recall carrying him back and laying him asleep in his new bed. We were both exhausted from playing battle of the wills. Seeing him asleep in the bed I had lovingly picked out gave me some sense of victory.

The next morning, I went to check on him and could not find him. I looked everywhere in our apartment. I called his name and there was no response. Then I started yelling his name. My home was completely quiet. My thoughts ranged from "He is playing hide-and-seek," to "He wandered outside!" I frantically ran through the apartment and went over the places I had already checked. I was about to lose it when I found him. He was in a deep sleep under his new bed.

In hindsight, I see that I was not kind to him that night. I may have prided myself on not saying mean things to Ricky but there was something just as bad in my opinion. The cruel tone in my voice. It had to be my way. The cute little toddler bed was not necessarily about him. It was about me being able to tell someone about Ricky's accomplishment. It was about me being able to show a picture and tell a story about how my cute little boy looks in his cute little big boy bed. Shortly after, I gave up my bed and put it in his room. I discovered he wasn't necessarily wanting to sleep next to me, he just wanted to be in a more comfortable bed. I get it now, sorry Ricky.

Sometimes life is cruel. We learn things too late. Maybe that is why grandparents are the way they are. Their kindness can be over the top because they wish they could have done things differently. Everyday awaits with new lessons and new opportunities. Each generation has wrestled with its own challenges. At the time of this writing, social media is the big change we are dealing with. I have not covered digital media or its danger to the development of infants and small children but I encourage you to look it up. I have read some studies that make me silently scream whenever I see a parent hand their phone off to their little one to stare at a screen. That was non-existent when I was a teen mom. The point is, keep yourself teachable. This book cannot possibly answer all your questions. My hope is that you always stay curious about what other resources are available to help you. When Ricky was little, I went to the library to find the books I needed. I read magazine articles, and got used to asking questions when I was with our doctor and other parents. With you in mind, I shared a list of helpful resources at the end of this book. You also have something that I did not - the internet. If you have access to the internet, you have quick information right at your finger tips!

You also have what some people call a "gut-instinct" or a "mother's intuition." Honestly, I believe it is God giving us a clue. Once when Ricky was one or two we were playing around in the kitchen. I dramatically scooped him up, flipped him up-side down and started to slap his back like I was saving him from something. Moments later a penny popped out of his mouth and onto the floor. I put him down quickly and checked him. He coughed a little and smiled but ultimately, he was fine. I stood there frozen. Another second later and that penny could have been lodged in his throat.

Saving my son's life, let's mark that as a milestone too.

I believe everyone does the best they can with what they know at the time. Motherhood is going to have some tough days. Choose a time when you are in a good place and write a letter to yourself to read when you are having a bad day.

If this is difficult for you, maybe you can ask someone that believes in you to write you an encouraging letter.

UNPLANNED

6

Face to Face

L ife was starting to stabilize. After a couple of years at the insurance agency I knew I could not be there forever. A hunger for something more started to awaken in me and push me to take a risk. I started thinking about the possibility of going to college. I set myself up to meet with a counselor at my local community college and before I knew it I was enrolling. Leaving a steady pay and health insurance in exchange for the unknown was a little scary. I remember being anxious about breaking the news to my boss. She gave an 18-year-old with little experience a wonderful chance to grow professionally and I respected her for that. The company had been so good to me. It was a small business with a family atmosphere and I felt like I was letting them down by leaving. My boss was sad to see me go, but I also remember seeing pride in her eyes. She knew it was a risk I had to take.

My mom is a risk-taker. I know this is where I get it from. Even with all her limitations, I have admired her courage and tenacity. As a young adult, she waved goodbye to her home country and ventured into another, whose language or culture she did not know.

Recently on Mother's Day, she bravely opened up to me about the hardships of her upbringing and missing her mother's death. There were stories I had never heard before. Once she started to tell her stories, it was like opening a floodgate, and every week more stories would come. My mom described what it felt like to take a risk by leaving Mexico, how she felt unwanted by her siblings and why she never married. She even told me of the time her mother sent her sister away to a home for girls because she coudn't control her. Sound familiar? I had compassion on her. All I could do was listen. When it seemed like she had arrived at a safe place to rest her soul, I would tell her how proud I was of her for sharing her stories. It occurred to me that most likely, she had never heard those words before.

In my eyes, her courage is better than the cape of a superhero. I know that my mom is not perfect. My way to honor her is to highlight the good. Her legacy is her generosity. It is the way she allows children to draw out her kindness. She passed on to me an awareness of God and I am grateful. It is a legacy I will continue to build upon.

I can see now, that leaving the security of a job to go to school was a risk that would pay off. I just did not know it then. Once the college processed all my paperwork, I learned that I had qualified for financial aid and all the necessary pieces started to fall into place. My mom's support to help care for Ricky, made going to school and picking up a part time job possible. We both made sacrifices to make this opportunity work for our family and I was so grateful.

Just to think, a few years earlier I was getting by as an average student with no interest in furthering my education. My motivation was low, and I was not a strong reader. In college, however, something clicked in me. It was not the college itself, rather my reason for being there became my motivation. There was that quiet strength arising in me again. I needed to push forward for my family's sake. Being in college was a true gift for someone like me and I found out how much I wanted to be there.

Somewhere along the way, I believed the lie that I was not college material. Even though high school tried to prepare me for it, college was a foreign idea. Some school wants me to leave home, the only home I know, to spend money that I don't have and leave my mom to fend for herself? It was easy then to believe college was not for me. I didn't realize there were other ways and believing the lie limited me. I knew that how I managed this opportunity would affect our future. I used every study trick I could find and spent long hours at the library. I took full advantage of their computer and study labs. Laziness and excuses were not an option! I was open to the possibilities of what could be. Once I started to overcome small challenges I started to wonder, "What else is possible?" I was being empowered all over again.

On my way to college one morning, in a borrowed beat up Toyota, I saw a friend at the bus stop. I knew him from high school and occasionally we rode the bus together. He was a jokester, always smiling and fun to be around. I offered him a ride and he hopped right in. We talked about all kinds of things including God. I wondered if this was an answer to a simple prayer I had made several weeks prior.

Weeks earlier, I had been flipping through the channels on TV first thing in the morning. I came across a woman with a raspy voice telling stories. She was easy to relate to because she spoke about life and faith, she kept it real. Watching her became part of my morning routine and before I knew it, my heart was being affected by her stories in a good way. It was like something in my heart was coming alive when she spoke. I felt like I needed to connect to the faith community again, I just did not know how. I managed to spit out a simple prayer for help and let it be.

Taking my friend to school that day turned out to be an answer to my prayer for sure. As we talked, he made an open invitation to visit his church. No pressure. By then, I was convinced that this was no coincidence. There were different ways God was getting my attention all along. My friend's invitation was indeed an answer to my humble prayer.

"I had been so strong for so long. It became impossible to keep it together anymore."

There are experiences in life that cause us to be aware of God and sensitive to issues of faith. We all have questions in our heart that seem to have no answer. Our hearts may cry, "God how could you let this happen? God why didn't you stop it? God, you should have..." I have come to the conclusion that God is big enough to handle our anger and our questions. Along in the journey there are times when our hopes and expectations are not met. We freak out and He understands. Our disappointments can lead to anger, which is not uncommon.

The God that the Bible speaks of is a loving Father. Sometimes He is misunderstood. He will continue to reach out to you because His love is unrelenting. Do you think this book might be God's way of wanting to get your attention? The God that I know does not give up.

There may have been choices that were made for us that were painful and of which we had no control. Maybe, we had parents or guardians that hurt us because that is all they knew. God is not the author of this type of pain and abuse. In the same breath, I can tell you He will not let this experience go to waste. He is an expert at turning things around and making something beautiful out of a hot mess. He is always looking to bring us into the safe place of His heart and His love. He is the purest and most selfless love we will ever experience.

Since I worked on Sundays, I made several attempts to visit on a week night. I would park my car across the street and wait. Ironically, no one had been coming on the nights someone was supposed to be there. Something in me would not let me give up. Finally, one cold

March night, the lights were on and I grabbed my chance.

I slipped in through the side door and sat in the back on purpose, so no one would notice me. I was not sure what to expect but I was there. As I sat there quietly, all the events of the last few years started to replay in my mind. I had been so strong for so long. It became impossible to keep it together anymore. The pain of all my decisions, both good and bad, had come alive in my soul. What I had done began to tear away from me. It was like my old identity was being stripped away and the events of my past were no longer who I was. The experience became extremely overwhelming. God was there. I was in a room full of strangers and it was increasingly harder to keep my cool. A simple knot in my throat turned into a complete explosion of emotions. Like a dam breaking, I felt the freedom to cry and let it all out. Without knowing the words to say, it felt like God was perfectly fine translating the language of my tears. I felt love wash over all my regrets. It was pain and gentleness all at once. Suddenly I had no fight in me to convince God that He was being kind to someone who wasn't worthy of a face to face meeting.

This experience with God was like the sun rising on a new day. When I first sat in my seat, the weight of the world was on me, but when I got up something in me had changed deeply. At the end of the night, I allowed the Pastor to pray for me and I took ownership of my faith. With my own words I simply stated what I had put my faith in: the death, burial and resurrection of Jesus for my sins. What seemed like a small decision, in an obscure place on a cold winter night, was the night I allowed love to change my life. Even though I was unsure about a lot of things, the one thing I was certain of was being loved and being forgiven. This experience with God's love placed a new light on my future. That was over 20 years ago.

I once read a story about a young guy who thought he had it goin' on! No one could tell him anything, even his dad. He made his dad give him money, so he could take off and live how he wanted to live. Things were good at home and yet, he thought his father owed him something. Pride drove this son far from home and his loved ones. He left home with a pocket full of money and he was living it up. With no curfew and no one to tell him what to do, he thought he had a sweet deal.

One day he found the money was gone and so were his friends. The only thing he had left to call his, were the clothes on his back and his own thoughts. Even though he ran from many things, the one thing he could not run away from was himself. Something happens when you find yourself at your lowest place. It becomes your breaking point. You are faced with a decision to choose between a hard heart or a humble one. This guy was so low that he was desperate enough to eat the food the animals ate on his dad's property. Only when he understood how wrong he had been, could he start his journey back home. He may have thought about how he was raised and realized that he was not meant to live like he was homeless, with no family.

Even though this guy was in a hurry to leave, the beautiful part of this story is that back home there was a dad still waiting for him to return home. Home is where love and forgiveness were waiting for him. The son was so ashamed that he did not think about expecting it. He thought if he could just get home, it would not even bother him one bit to come back as one of his dad's workers. This guy did not yet understand that a son is always a son.

This story is hundreds of years old and yet, it is my story too. Can you relate? It represents the condition of our heart. It is about what happens when we do things selfishly, without care of how it will affect someone else. From this frame of mind, it is difficult to receive good things from those that love us. We lose our sense of home.

Wherever you find yourself today, you can turn to God. You can make a choice to lay down your pride, selfishness or anything else that may be harming you and your loved ones. Look closely, I believe you will find God's mercy in your past and His grace in your present. His favor and goodness are even found in your future. It is because of His great love that we are found to be worthy. We are His loved ones.

Several weeks after this encounter, one of my college professors looked at me curiously. The kind of look someone gives you when they notice a change that they have not quite figured out yet.

"You look different," he commented. "Did you meet someone?"

I smiled and said softly, "Jesus."

He nodded slowly, "Good for you," he replied. I got the feeling that he did not relate but was glad to see me happy. It was easy for us to have this conversation on such a personal subject because we had been studying the book Living, Loving and Learning by Leo Buscaglia. After studying love for a class grade, I had met the true Author of the subject Himself in that little church on a cold winter night.

Plant good things

Let's compare life to a garden. Our thoughts, words and actions are like the seeds we plant. We feed ourselves and others out of that garden. This garden becomes our legacy.

A legacy is something we inherit and also something we pass on to our children. We may feel proud or ashamed of what has been passed on to us.

Can you name a few things you are choosing not to pass on to your children?

What are some things you would like to pass on?

UNPLANNED

7

It's Complicated

Paralyzed. That best describes how I felt about dating as a single mom. I was infatuated with the idea but not the work that it required.

Have you ever watched girls play double-dutch? There's that one girl doing that bouncing rock back and forth as she prepares to jump in. That was my love life and I was that girl. I made some attempts at dating but nothing serious.

I daydreamed about what it would be like to be in a loving relationship. Despite most of the real-life examples I saw, I had a knowing that it was possible. I am a hope junkie, I guess. One of my close high school friends had parents that were married and seemed to enjoy each other. They were affectionate with one another, laughed together and seemed to sincerely care about each other. Their example had a positive and lasting impact on me. It was not common but they showed me this kind of relationship did exist.

Nevertheless, the idea of actual dating was awkward for me. There were questions constantly occupying my mind:

"How soon do I tell a guy I have a son?"

"What if I don't say because I don't think it's going anywhere, and then it becomes serious?"

"What if he likes me, but isn't cool with a baby?"

"What if my son gets attached, but it doesn't work out?"

"How is it going to work with a boyfriend and my baby's father?"

This was an ongoing mental battle for me. For much of my time I was quite content in my singleness. Life was low-drama which was nice for a change. In addition to motherhood, I kept busy by going to school, working and being involved in church.

Occasionally, I went out. I don't remember going past one or two dates with someone. I felt protective of my son and made certain decisions to guard him. I was upfront with a guy about having a son and often found myself holding my breath, waiting for a reaction. Finding someone you want to be with can be hard. Finding someone when you have a child to look out for is complicated. One of the boundaries I set up for myself was that no one could meet my family right away. A few times though, it was impossible to avoid. I remember what it was like when my mom went on dates and there were certain things I did not want to repeat. I could not explain why, but watching her being affectionate with a man irritated me. I believe she had good intentions by including me but "family dates" were a bad idea.

When I was about nine years old a man came to take us out. My mom knew his sister and she must have thought he was a decent guy. While my mom was getting ready, he slipped a porn magazine out of a brown paper bag and exposed me to something my eyes should have never seen. He put his hand on my back and gave me a strange smile. In one millisecond, he went from decent guy to creepy guy. Frozen and confused, I couldn't say anything. Before much else could happen, my mom walked back into the room. Thank God that I had the boldness to speak up! I was able to tell her what he had shown me, and she immediately removed him from our home. We never saw him again. Looking back, I see that this moment taught me to be my son's protector.

Another reason to keep a guy away from my family is that I did not want my son to get attached to someone who was not going to stay in our lives. Watching my son get his heart broken because the relationship did not work out

> "I had boundaries in place to protect my son, but no plan to protect myself."

was not an option. Once, my mom dated a guy for a while and we all moved in together (another bad idea). I didn't always like seeing him and my mom together. He did make her happy though, so I went along with it. There were things that I did not like about him, more a matter of personal preferences but he was okay. After a year or so, when the relationship fell apart, he moved out and it broke my heart. Considering I did not "feel" attached to him, I did not expect to feel sad when he left. He was not even my favorite person and, yet I felt abandoned by him.

Even though I held my mom's mistakes against her for a time, I managed to make several of my own. While I was strict about protecting Ricky, I wasn't the greatest at protecting myself.

One time I agreed to go out with someone who worked late at night. He traveled with his job and I met him at his hotel room in order to go out. What was I thinking? He was not from my circle of acquaintances, I did not know him previously or knew anyone that did. This was before you could Google anyone or know them on social media. Thankfully nothing bad happened but this could have been a dangerous situation. If something horrible would have happened to me, no one would have known where I was or who I was with.

Another time, I felt comfortable enough to go to someone's house alone for dinner because this time I did know him. Still we were alone, and I left myself vulnerable. Again. I admit, from time to time I felt lonely. Loneliness can lead us to do things we normally would not do.

I had boundaries in place to protect my son, but no plan to protect myself. Based on my last relationship, I watched for red flags. I looked for things like jealousy, excessive drinking, and the pressure to have sex. Some might think I did not drink for religious reasons, in fact I had convinced myself of the same. In hindsight, I can see that I avoided drinking because I did not want to lose control. I did not want to leave myself in a position where someone could take advantage of me or that I would do something I could not remember. It wasn't worth it.

"Love was starting to look like a minefield."

Sex became out of the question for me. I know that's not a decision everyone feels they can make but it is possible. Around that time, I had read a magazine article about a woman that decided to stop having sex. Even though she was no longer a virgin, she was going to wait to have sex until she got married. I was surprised to learn that people actually did that. Until I read her story I had not realized that waiting was an option. It is an actual thing that people practice called celibacy. Just like some go to great lengths to be physically fit or maintain a healthy lifestyle, some have learned the discipline of celibacy. I thought I had to give in to the expectations of others. As is typical with women, I equated sex with love. I also associated it with trust and commitment. Let's face it though. Guys are not wired the same way, especially not the guys that were in my age group. My relationship goals were not going to come by the drama attached to a sexual relationship. Let's be honest there is a certain level of drama that comes with sex. It is a physical act with emotional ties. I wanted to be held and loved. I wanted someone to look in my eyes and think I was amazing without the promise of immediate sex. That is also a two-way street. Even though sex was created for pleasure, just like everything else, it has a proper time and place. I choose not to hand over the keys of my car to a five-year-old child just because they are cute and can say "Vroom! Vroom!" It doesn't mean they won't ever drive, it just means it's not time yet. Like the other big decisions I was making, this decision was made with our future in mind. Waiting became a matter of self-control. It became about the healthy relationship I was preparing myself for. I was still figuring out who I was and what I wanted. There was no room for clouded judgment. Truthfully, it was the last thing I needed. Then of course there were the risks of STDs and getting pregnant again. Anyone quick to get physical, showed me that he would have been that way with plenty of others. A man with no self-control? Pass! I had decided I was worth protecting.

I was scared to jeopardize all the progress I had made so far. Love was starting to look like a minefield. I also did not want to end up a bitter, "I don't need a man" type of woman that chose to remain single out of fear. This part of my life was going to be complicated. The question was, who was going to be worth the work?

I know this chapter may not be where you are right now. If you are, how complicated would you rate it on a scale of 1-10?

If you do find yourself single, can you list two boundaries you could set for yourself that would protect both you and your child?

Aside from a dating relationship, what loving relationships do you have in your life? (Ex. mom, dad, sister, brother, guardian, friend, etc)?

You might be among the ones that still have a romantic relationship with their baby's father. What do you appreciate about him the most?

8

Loving Again

Did I mention I was really diggin' this low-drama life? I wanted to be in a loving relationship, but I was not interested in anything sketchy. Sometimes singleness felt like it was lasting forever and at the same time there was no rush to be in love. I had not met anyone that I was willing to take a risk for again. Then Marc happened, and my plans were forever altered.

A few months after I started going to church, I noticed a young guy that came to visit for a special event. He was unquestionably easy on the eyes. I mean, I was in church, but I wasn't blind! For an unguarded moment, this dude held my attention. The church was celebrating an anniversary and he came to volunteer as a camera guy. Almost as fast as I noticed him, I stopped myself. I quickly put my excitement in check and thought, "I am not here for that!" There was a determination in me to get myself to a healthy place without any distractions, not even a good-looking one.

Fast forward almost two years and I was enrolled at the church's Bible school. It was small which made it easy to get to know the other students. All of them were married except for myself and one other student, Marc. I was vaguely aware of who he was. Although he was a year ahead of me, he had flunked a class which meant he had to repeat it with our group. This dropped him right into one of my classes where I would see him one night a week for a whole semester. Since we were the only single people there, it was immediately awkward. I could feel the eyes of the other students on us, almost like their eyebrows were dancing with delight. They were sweet people with good intentions, but it felt like their cupid's arrow was drawn. I became more guarded.

Marc was quiet like me and I made note of his kind smile. Taller than me, he carried a strong appearance, and yet I did not find myself being intimidated. Not only was he easy on the eyes, I found myself being drawn to him in a way that scared me a little. There was something I could not explain.

We got to know each other slowly. Over the next few months, Marc asked me out several times. With much excitement I would say yes. Yet once I had time to think about what that meant, I would get nervous and cancel. Between church and our circle of friends, we began to see each other more frequently. He was gentle and persistent, never pressuring me. His approach was different than what I had known before.

One night during a break at Bible school, I walked through the church to get to the restroom which was on the other side. The lights in the sanctuary were dim but I could see one person praying alone at the front. That person's dedication was such a beautiful sight to me. It deserved the utmost respect. Not wanting to interrupt that sacred moment, I did my best to move by quietly. After I returned, I stopped to privately talk to the pastor who was also one of the main teachers. Actually, I needed Marc's phone number so I could respond to his latest invitation. I was intent on being discreet, so the other students would not find out. While I waited, Marc walked out from the sanctuary, and I was stunned. I realized that he was the one praying alone. This might sound crazy, but in that moment, I heard God whisper, "It's only a matter of time." I tried to act normal, but I was in a state of shock. If you want a visual, think "a deer caught in headlights" look.

I was being confronted with the risk of loving again and it triggered some next-level anxiety and fear. What if it didn't work out? What if I got hurt? What if this hurt my son? Although I had hopes for a relationship, I found myself reacting out of my past fears. I had to wrestle with the infamous "what ifs" in my head.

The first time I kept my word to go out with Marc happened because the invitation was for all of us. He had bought tickets for Ricky, my mom and myself to a church event. It felt safe because I was steppin' out with all my crew. There was three of us and one of him. Still I questioned what I was doing. I was even breaking my own "no family dates" rule!

"His approach was different than what I had known before."

I guess because church was our common ground, I thought it would be okay. This eventually eased me into our first official date, just him and I. It was a little nerve-racking. We had that first-date awkwardness going on but once we started talking at the restaurant, we couldn't stop. We relaxed and the world around us fell away. Marc and I laughed and listened intently to each other's stories. By the end of dinner, I thought maybe I'd like to do this again. He took me home and we still could not stop talking. We sat in the driveway for another one hour, perhaps two. We each found the boldness to speak from the heart. If we were not on the same page as it concerned our futures, then we didn't want to waste each other's time. Marc spoke of the things my heart had been hoping for but I tried not to react. I was trying to take it all in when suddenly I felt the presence of God flood the car. It was like waves of peace I had not ever felt before. I did my best to play it cool but that night something had changed. When our date came to an end, I walked into my house and told my mom to start saving for a dress. We exchanged girlish giggles and left it there.

When Marc and I started officially dating in the spring of 1999, it was such a sweet time. It was innocent and awkward, even clumsy at times. We were real with one another upfront, both serious and silly. We found that our views on dating were the same because we understood our lives had purpose. Long conversations led us to get to know each other and to develop the friendship within our relationship relatively quickly. Knowing we had mutual friends and interests helped a great deal as well.

Ricky was four years old around that time. He was old enough to understand and I needed to be extra careful. Slowly, Marc was introduced to my family as a "friend" from church. I watched him carefully with Ricky and looked for red flags. Was he short tempered? Was he mean to my son? Was there anything that seemed off? I looked for any signs that would show me if Marc would be the same person when he thought no one was watching as when he knew they were. When they would play together, I would study them. I also watched for Ricky's responses to Marc. They both looked comfortable and genuinely happy to be around one another. I saw Marc enjoy being involved in Ricky's life. Equally, I saw Ricky excited to have a man to look up to. When they were together, the honesty of his big Kool-Aid smile spoke volumes.

> "His sense of hope made me confront my fear of being disappointed."

One day, Ricky and I were having a teachable moment and I was explaining the concept of trust. I told him it meant "to believe what someone says." He turned to me with his sweet brown eyes and in his adorable little voice he dropped a bomb, "Do you believe Marc?" It rocked me. That question haunted me for days. Could I trust Marc? I was feeling unsure and still in the process of sorting out all the new emotions that came with his presence in my life. What I could identify was fear trying to grip me. Like a whisper to my heart I heard the words, "Trust in the Lord." Suddenly I felt a rush of peace come over me. Those words did something to the deepest parts of my soul that settled my insecurities.

Ricky had a way of saying unexpected things that were like revelations. Then there were times that we were quickly reminded of his age. Like that one Sunday when we had Marc over for dinner. We were eating and joking around. At a break in the conversation Ricky began to study Marc's face, then mine. He had made an observation he was proud to share with everyone present, "Mommy, you have a mustache." Umm, what? Mortified. Yes, that is the word which describes that moment perfectly! Marc thought it was hilarious. On another occasion, Marc, Ricky and I were playing in the living room and Ricky asked, "Are you gonna be my daddy?" Crickets. How do you recover from either of those scenarios? You remember to breathe. At four years old, Ricky was easily distracted. One of us managed to point out how cool his toy was and the "daddy" conversation was put on the shelf, or at least we thought. It felt like we dodged a bullet.

Marc was exactly the kind of man I needed, he created a safe place for me. Without words, I had the sense that he had my back. I never felt pressured to be physically affectionate or to do anything else I didn't want to do. Still, I found myself being resistant to what our relationship could mean. It was probably a few months into dating before we even started to hold hands. His selfless affection challenged my ideas and past experiences. His kindness made me think seriously about what it takes to have a solid relationship. His sense of hope made me confront my fear of being disappointed.

Shortly before knowing Marc, I prayed something along the lines of "God, I know I might overlook the man that you send my way. Please help me to see him when he comes into my life." I know that God showed up in this part of my life, too. Would you believe me if I told you that he turned out to be the camera guy that caught my attention a few years earlier?

Marc was soft spoken, and intense in a calm sort of way. Please don't misunderstand. His quietness and low-key personality was not a sign of weakness. There was a noticeable confidence in how he carried himself. He was aware of his power, yet felt no need to display it carelessly. He showed me that a man could be tender without losing his masculinity. That was intriguing to me. He was also reserved in public but once he started talking about his dreams he had plenty to say. The way he passionately spoke about his dreams felt like permission to honor my own. His excitement was contagious. Over time I settled into the sound of his voice when he said my name. It felt like home. Marc looked at me like I was the only one in the room. I admit sometimes it was uncomfortable. Not because it was creepy but because he was making me feel worthy of love. Maybe, he thought I was amazing? His consistent love was starting to convince me that maybe I was. It felt like he saw something good in me that I was uncomfortable seeing for myself. The idea of loving again started to grow on me. Aside from being attracted to him, in his presence I got used to feeling protected and valuable in a healthy way. I was hooked.

When Marc asked me to marry him, he blew my mind. My family, Marc and I had been together at a church service. Toward the end of our gathering, the pastor called him to the platform to read something "special" that he had prepared. Moments later I was called up front as well. Marc started to read and before I knew it, in a room full of people he was on one knee. I don't remember hearing actual words. Only after seeing Marc look up at me with a ring in his hand did I put the pieces together. This man was proposing! The whole church lost it like their favorite team had scored the winning touchdown. On the inside, I was a crazy mix of emotions. Like when you settle into the wildest ride at the theme park. You're scared because you don't know what's coming but you know it's going to be awesome! I don't remember words coming out of my mouth, but I do remember that I managed to shake my head yes. Wow. Were we really doing this?

At the end of the night, there were plenty of congratulatory hugs and excitement from everyone. Marc kissed me goodnight and I was on my way home with this foreign object on my finger. For several days I could not stop staring at my left hand. Upside down, right-side up, in the mirror, up close, far away. My family was so happy. With all the commotion Ricky thought that was the wedding! I had to explain to my sweet boy what had just happened. Then I got to break the news that he would get to be the ring bearer on our actual wedding day and he was thrilled. I was so happy to see his genuine excitement.

It may have sounded too soon for some. Since we had been upfront with each other from the beginning, and ran in the same circle of friends, our relationship developed quickly. We kept it real with each other which created a strong level of trust and confidence. These things combined led us to a deep love that went beyond our initial physical attraction. We were surrounded by loving people who did all they could to make sure our marriage would have success. We took a year long engagement and planned for a simple wedding. Our focus through

> "He showed me that a man could be tender without losing his masculinity."

much of that year was dedicated to working through communication and relationship building. We were able to get our hands on a workbook called Preparing for Marriage. As is common with new love, in the beginning of our relationship we were looking at everything with rose-colored glasses. This workbook forced us to talk about money, sex and communication. For several weeks we would meet to go over what we learned and how we had answered the questions about our expectations. Who would pay the bills? How many times a week would we have sex? How many kids did we want? We also had to take a closer look at each of our family histories and what we were expecting from our married life together. It made for some intense conversations but from that we walked away with clarity. In addition to help from our pastors, we also asked another couple to mentor us through the process. They shared their personal experiences and how they dealt the issues that came with married life. Since Marc had a divorce in his past and I had Ricky, we were intentional about doing all we could to make this work.

We also made a decision that would be a game changer for us. Since we both carried a prior sexual history and the heartbreak that came with it, we relied on our faith to show us a better way. For this to work for us, that meant we were choosing to wait on sex until our wedding day. I know that sounds old-fashioned, but it was what we needed. It was what God was asking of us. This commitment was not easy. At its root, waiting is an issue of self-control. Toward the end of our engagement, we especially struggled in this area. Staying up late nights alone to work on wedding preparations had put us in a vulnerable place. There were times we crossed some of the limits we had set. We had to face our weaknesses and set our boundaries back up again. That and sending Marc home to a number of cold showers!

"Our marriage has been about loving and learning in an intentional way."

In May of 2000 on a rainy spring day, our wedding had finally arrived. It was a day filled with joy and anxiety, make-up and attitudes, excitement and peace. With the amazing support of our family and friends, we publicly declared our promises to one another. In the presence of God and our guests, we were laying out the vision we had for our future. In addition to the wedding gifts we received, people gave of their time and resources along the way to help us pull it all together. Their words, both written and spoken, encouraged our hearts so much. Our wedding had become a symbol of healing, restoration and joy. That day Marc and I felt like we could conquer the world!

After all the excitement of the day Marc, Ricky and I snuck away for some privacy. It was time to remind Ricky about being away for our honeymoon trip. We ran through the details of who he would be with and when we would return. Completely unscripted, Ricky asked Marc, "Does this mean I can call you Daddy now?" The conversation that we had put on the shelf was in our faces again. To say that we were caught off guard is an understatement. Until then we had not discussed that topic since Ricky's first mention of it. Basically, we had avoided it. We did not want to force what Ricky would call Marc. Personally, I wanted it to come from him naturally and it did. In the quietness of that room we shared a tender moment that I will never forget. From that day forward, not only had Marc become my husband, he had become Ricky's dad. It was the icing on the cake!

Speaking of icing on the cake, naturally the wedding day led to the wedding night. The wait was over. Neither Marc nor I had to leave at the end of the night and he did not have to force himself into a cold shower. It was both a relief and a pleasure. As we prepared for married life, Marc and I had been learning each other's communication styles and discovering our boundaries. I know that might not sound very sexy. However, the love and respect that we had been building up to that point, crossed over into our sex life. Great sex doesn't just happen. You must communicate and put into practice what you have agreed on. I am aware that I am competing with books and movies that tell it all. What I can tell you is that it has been awesome to wake up in the morning and be happy with the man I am sharing a bed with. The threat of violence and humiliation was completely absent. This too, became part of my healing.

That was many years ago. Life with Marc has been a mixture of laughter and laundry, night time coffee and learning to work through disagreements. We live in the belief that one another is worth it. We are also crazy enough to believe that you can take pleasure in the person you marry and that growing old together is possible. As best we could, we have carefully helped each other unpack the baggage from our past. Marc and I have come a long way. There have been plenty of healing tears and praying through. More importantly, we have enjoyed our life together. We are a team. Our marriage has been about loving and learning in an intentional way. The life we created has given us a platform to encourage others, both privately and publicly. This has been a big leap for me from being a runaway, hopeless hot mess. I can tell you with a clear conscience that anything is possible.

Matters of the heart

Love does not automatically guarantee a life free of conflict. When we love we allow ourselves to be vulnerable and that means we can get hurt, even from the person who has the best intentions. It is always a good idea to work on our emotional health and communications skills. Think about all the things that make a relationship work.

If you are in no rush to be in a dating relationship right now, what can you do to prepare for a future relationship?

What kind of qualities do you want in the person you will share your life and parenting responsibilities with?

Is there a married couple that you can be open with and get advice from?

9

Just Getting Started

L ife changed on us, again. Marc stepped into the role of a new husband and father. As a new wife, I was adjusting to shared parenting responsibilities. Additionally, there were new in-laws to get to know, as well as learning how to maintain the friendships we had before were a married couple. This was not a fairy-tale ending. We professed, "I do" and we were really just getting started. As all our lives merged together it was not easy. The first six months proved to be the toughest on me.

Ricky had to navigate a whole new world, too. He now had two people to play with and sing him silly songs instead of one. He also had two people keep him in check when he thought not listening was an option. Probably not his favorite part as a kid. If one of us was sick or too tired, the other one could step up. We were a team. Marc and I did bedtime stories, funny accents, and road trips. By now you know I keep it real, so I am obligated to tell you there was also yelling, frustration, saying "no" and being challenged in new ways. These were unchartered waters for us all.

This new change also meant, my mom was no longer my right hand. Getting married was exciting but moving away from her was harder than I had anticipated. So many decisions were being made because of our new family dynamic. We got it wrong sometimes. What we got right, was the desire to always do better for the sake of each other. I can tell you our family has been soaked in prayer. Sometimes the prayers were long, then there were the prayers that sounded more like a one-word cry for help. God was used to the sound of our voices.

We started to create our own family traditions, like family dinners. Growing up, the work schedules our parents had caused this practice to be was lost. Through Marc, I learned how to cook rice the Puerto Rican way. As a teenager I had several failed attempts at rice but this was now the kind that people actually wanted to eat. I would watch him move in the kitchen and carefully select his spices. He would taste as he cooked and kept at it until he was satisfied. Marc would do all the major work and I followed up behind him to clean. I loved to watch Marc take pleasure over being creative in the kitchen. His cooking wasn't just food. It became his way to serve us and express his love. He shifted my thinking from seeing cooking as a burden and instead it became a delight. Looking back, it was also an answer to prayer. At that time in my life my cooking was not anything to brag about. Marc changed that too! Our dinners became a sacred time to share a meal and our hearts, without interruption. The television was turned off most times and no one would answer the phone during our dinner time. Being together around the table became that important to us. Ricky would help clean up afterwards and we made it a team effort.

One ingredient of a successful team is good listening. Love does not automatically qualify us to be an influence in our child's life. It is about the time we spend with them and how we listen to their hearts, not just their words. Whoever or whatever our child spends the most time around will be able to influence them the most. It is through the time and attention that we give them which enables us to have an impact on their life. Our kids want to know "Do you see me?"

Since I am a fairly laid-back person, I frequently get asked, "Do you ever get mad?" Almost always, I respond by telling them to ask my son. He knows the loud part of me. The reason is that I have dreams for my son. I want better for him than I had. I was especially determined that he would have a better life than his biological father. For all those times I struggled with my worth I wanted him to know that he was great. For the many times I held myself back I wanted him to know that he could work hard and achieve something. Sometimes my determination back-fired and I see now that I was too hard on him.

We did not get a "happily ever after" like we see in the movies, we got something better. In our errors, we experienced forgiveness and in our failures, we found grace. We discovered how high and deep love was. In fact, we are still discovering it. As long as our pride does not get in the way then we are good. We have our faith to keep us grounded as well. Truly, if God had not stepped in I do not know where we would be. We did not need Him just once but countless times. God showed up as our Comforter when our hearts were broken, and He showed up as our Provider when we were in need. Let's face it, sometimes life is messy.

The longer I live the more love-driven I become. Ricky is a young adult now and he survived being raised by a teen mom. It is still my heart's pleasure to introduce him to someone and say, "This is my son." Now, he has his own story to tell. Like me, Ricky was around two the last time he saw his father. We understand that life does not always go as planned. More so, we recognize that in life we will find the support of family, friends and even strangers along the way. Like the experience at the playground, in life there will be challenges. Thankfully, we have these three we can count on: faith, hope and love.

Most likely, you are at the beginning of motherhood. You too, are just getting started. Whether you choose to keep your baby or give another family hope through the blessing of adoption, you will experience a level of sacrifice you have never known before. You may find that staying with your baby's father is a healthy choice or perhaps you are being faced with raising your baby as a single parent. Either way, do not allow the circumstances to talk you out of the powerful future that is still ahead of you. You may not feel comfortable in your own skin today. From experience I can tell you that if you choose to learn and grow, one day you will.

My hope is that you'll give yourself a chance. Even with a child on your hip, give yourself the opportunity to pursue the God-given dreams that are tucked away in your heart. I believe that your future is bright. Don't be afraid to shine!

This book could have easily been called:

Messy and Beautiful

Reintoducing Hope

The Girl Who Got Up Again

Maybe, those are the stories you were meant to write. It was not until almost publishing this book that I gave thought to the other 505,487 teen moms that delivered a baby the same year that Ricky was born. I was so focused on not being a part of the statistics that I forgot to have compassion on their stories. The other fighters, survivors and victors.

You are not just a number dear heart. Your story matters. Is life messy right now? You are not alone. Feel the pain of the moment. Then hand it over to God because He is not shocked and certainly not afraid of it. Own your part in it. Work through it with Him, then say goodbye to the mess. You can make it! You must want to make it and take actions accordingly.

Also, do not forget to laugh along the way! Life will not always go as planned and it will be important to have a good sense of humor. If you feel you don't have one, find a way to work on it! We cannot afford to always take things so seriously. Laughter helps us to break out of the places we feel stuck in. If you look at my list of labels on paper, there is a stigma attached that I could have gotten stuck in.

- Hispanic
- 17
- Runaway
- Teen mom
- Government assistance
- Dating violence survivor
- Fatherless
- Latch-key kid

It is natural to quickly judge and put me into a stereo-type. Once you move past that, I trust you will see the story of a young woman that overcame. Someone who did not stay stuck and let the statistics limit her.

What are the limits you are facing? The antidote for a limit is a goal. You must have goals for yourself. Some that you can accomplish short term, like in the next six months to one year. Think. What do you want for yourself? For your child? What will it take to get there? Success does not just happen. Begin to think about where you want to be five years from now. Don't worry about how hard it looks to get there. All you have is time. No matter what, you will be somewhere five years from now. Why not have a say in how it turns out? The healing and growing that will happen during this process will occur in layers. Why not allow these difficult times to prepare you for greater things? What if the challenges you are facing, are really meant to unleash the warrior in you.

I believe you can make it. You are not alone. Your life is not over, it is just going to be different than you imagined it.

Dear young mom,

You have an amazing life ahead. Life is not going to be easy but every effort to move forward will be worth it. I believe you are brave, and you have what it takes to make it. your dreams are still possible, you will just have to travel a different road now. Whatever it took to write Unplanned - you were 100% worth it!

Much love,
Blanca

P.S. Here are other life changing books for you to check out:

A Young Woman After God's Own Heart by Elizabeth George

Be Angry But Don't Blow It by Lisa Bevere

Boundaries by Dr. Henry Cloud and Dr. John Townsend

If Not For the Grace of God by Joyce Meyer

In Love and In Danger: A Teen's Guide to Breaking Free of Abusive Relationships by Barrie Levy

Living, Loving and Learning by Leo Buscaglia

Loving Our Kids on Purpose by Danny Silk

Rich Dad, Poor Dad by Robert Kiyosaki

Shattered Into Beautiful by Jeannie Scott Smith

The Dream Giver by Bruce Wilkinson

The Wait by Devon Franklin and Meagan Good

Unstoppable by Cynthia Kersey

What To Expect When You Are Expecting by Heidi Murkoff and Sharon Mazel

You Are Not What You Weigh by Lisa Bevere

Your Voice, Your Choice by April Hernandez Castillo

*The Bible (if you are new to the Bible, stick to Psalms, Proverbs and the Book of John)

For more information, resources or updated social media platforms visit our website bethebridgesc.org

If you would like to share how this book has impacted you please contact Blanca via email at myunplannedstory@gmail.com

Please help share the word on social media using the hashtag
#myunplannedstory

90471705R00055

Made in the USA
Columbia, SC
08 March 2018